Text copyright © 2002 by Nord-Süd Verlag AG, Gossau Zürich, Switzerland.
First published in Switzerland under the title *Der Regenbogenfisch lernt zählen*.
English translation copyright © 2002 by North-South Books Inc., New York

First published in Great Britain, Australia, and New Zealand in 2002 by
North-South Books, an imprint of Nord-Süd Verlag AG, Gossau Zürich, Switzerland.

A CIP catalogue record for this book is available from The British Library.

ISBN 0-7358-1717-0 (trade edition) 10 9 8 7 6 5 4 3 2 1

Printed in Italy

For more information about our books, and the authors and artists
who create them, visit our web site: www.northsouth.com

MARCUS PFISTER

Rainbow Fish
1, 2, 3

NORTH-SOUTH BOOKS
NEW YORK / LONDON

How many  yellow scales
does Rainbow Fish have?

Can you count one orange starfish, too?

How many ⬤ orange scales
does Rainbow Fish have?

Can you count two
purple clamshells, too?

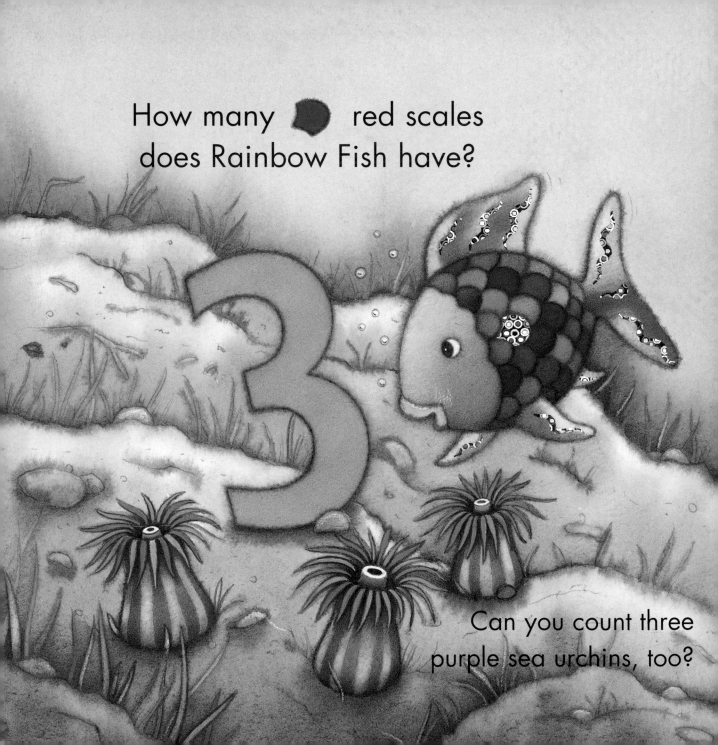

How many red scales does Rainbow Fish have?

Can you count three purple sea urchins, too?

How many 🟢 green scales
does Rainbow Fish have?

Can you count four orange-and-yellow sea horses, too?

How many  pink scales
does Rainbow Fish have?

Can you count five blue conch shells, too?

How many  purple scales
does Rainbow Fish have?

Can you count
six green leaves, too?

How many  blue scales
does Rainbow Fish have?

Can you count
seven blue
fish, too?

8

How many purple purple scales does Rainbow Fish have?

Can you count eight green prickly plants, too?

How many  blue scales
does Rainbow Fish have?

Can you count nine orange crabs, too?

How many  silver scales does Rainbow Fish have?

10

Can you count ten pretty bubbles, too?